HILLARY CLINTON HAIKU

HER RISE TO POWER, SYLLABLE BY SYLLABLE, PANTSUIT BY PANTSUIT

VERA G. SHAW

ILLUSTRATIONS BY EMMY REIS

TWELVE

NEW YORK BOSTON

Twelve
Hachette Book Group
1290 Avenue of the Americas
New York, NY 10104

www.HachetteBookGroup.com

Printed in the United States of America

RRD-C

First Edition: October 2015

10 9 8 7 6 5 4 3 2 1

Twelve is an imprint of Grand Central Publishing.
The Twelve name and logo are trademarks of Hachette Book Group, Inc.

The Hachette Speakers Bureau provides a wide range of authors for speaking events. To find out more, go to www.hachettespeakersbureau.com or call (866) 376-6591.

The publisher is not responsible for websites (or their content) that are not owned by the publisher.

Library of Congress Cataloging-in-Publication Data

Shaw, Vera G.
    Hillary Clinton haiku : her rise to power, syllable by syllable, pantsuit by pantsuit / by Vera G. Shaw ; illustrations by Emmy Reis. — First edition.
        pages cm
    Includes bibliographical references.
    ISBN 978-1-4555-3167-7 (hardcover) — ISBN 978-1-4555-3164-6 (ebook)   1. Clinton, Hillary Rodham—Poetry.   I. Reis, Emmy.   II. Title.
    PS3619.H39465A6 2015
    811'.6—dc23
                                                                                2015025046

Contents

We often confuse

images with reali-

ties, words with actions.

—Hillary Rodham,
Thesis, Wellesley College, 1969

Introduction

From youthful ambition to imminent world domination, it is incontestable that Hillary Rodham Clinton's life is the stuff of poetry. And in this high-speed internet age of TMI (Too Much Information), this age of the listicle and the tweet, this age of TL; DR (Too Long; Didn't Read), why would—nay, why *should*—anyone peruse anything longer than seventeen syllables (or, you know, thereabouts)?

Therefore, I am pleased to present to you *Hillary Clinton Haiku: Her Rise to Power, Syllable by Syllable, Pantsuit by Pantsuit*, a collection that distills the essential details of HRC where thousands of articles and biographies fall short—or, rather, long.

I believe (and I think soon you will too) that the haiku—a traditional form of Japanese verse that is both simple and elegant—is the perfect vehicle to honor the simple elegance of the preeminent politician of our time.

It is my sincerest hope that you enjoy this clarifying and expeditious read. God bless you, and God bless America.

—Vera G. Shaw

Glossary of Terms

Cankle A condition wherein any gracefully tapering transition from the calf portion of a leg and the ankle portion is virtually impossible to discern to the human eye.

FLOAR First Lady of Arkansas (AR).

FLOTUS First Lady of the United States.

LMAO What kids these days call "Laughing My Ass Off." (Pronounced here as each letter: L-M-A-O.)

LOL What the kids these days call "Laughing Out Loud." (Pronounced here as one syllable.)

Pantsuit A fashionable ensemble worn by women (i.e., Hillary) consisting of color-coordinated trousers and jacket.

POTUS President of the United States (i.e., ~~Hillary~~ Bill Clinton).

Scrunchie Fabric-covered elastic device made for holding back and/or up human (i.e., Hillary) hair.

Y Why (as in, "Oh God, why?!").

YOLO You Only Live Once.

I

Lil Hillary

Astronaut Hillary

Ma bent to Pa's needs.

Hill hoped to rocket outta

there. NASA: "No girls."

Lil Hill's Look

Coke-bottle plastic

frames, framed by blond locks, stubborn

as she would end up...

Lil Hillary

Meeting a Bully

Ma says fight back. When

Lil Hillary wins: "I can

play with the boys now."

"The Best Tool You Can Give a Child Is a Shovel"

"**H**ow you gonna dig

yourself out of this?" Dad says.

Literal Hill thinks...

Lil Hillary

Losing the [Class] Election

Lil Hill, don't worry.

Those Park Ridge school-kid voters

just do not know squat.

 7

Wellesley Hillary

President at last!

(Of a class of debutantes.)

Hippie Hill in slacks.

Lil Hillary

Meeting Bill at Yale Law

A south wind blew north.

Who was this charming man?! thought

each girl on campus.

 9

A Modest Proposal

The Lake District at

twilight finds Bill asking Hill

to be his wife. "Nah."

Lil Hillary

An Eventual "I Do"

Hill refused to nix

her name, remained Hillary

Diane Rodham, Esq.

2

Lil Rock Hillary

Gubernatorial

It sounds like just what

it is. A whole lot of nuts...

and for what... for what...

FLOAR Hair

Hitched First Lady of

Arkansas dreams of campaigns,

buys headbands instead.

Lil Rock Hillary

FLOAR Days

Bill plays governor

happily in the mansion,

Hill's job pays the bills.

FLOAR Duties

Committee meetings,

Easter egg hunts ... Where has it

gone, my ambition?

Lil Rock Hillary

An Equal Marriage

Partner at law firm!

Make more bling than Bill! Who wears

the real pantsuit now?

Baby Billary

Governor Clinton

comes to Lamaze. H. Rodham

pops out a lil girl.

Lil Rock Hillary

Governor Bill's Dalliances

What a tall glass of

water, thought quite a few Lil

Rock women. (Scandal?)

Hillary Stands by Her Man

Because kids without

dads are "precarious boats

in turbulent seas."

Lil Rock Hillary

3

FLOTUS Hillary

Hill-Billies

"Never thought the long-haired, bearded guy I married would be president."

The Wicked Witches of the East Wing

Preceded by Barb

Bush; succeeded by Laura.

Much too much Texas.

FLOTUS Hillary

POTUS on Hillary

"FLOTUS can hammer out consensus. FLOTUS can get things done," quoth Prez.

"I'm Undaunted in My Quest to Amuse Myself by Constantly Changing My Hair"

A bob? An updo?

A bun? A twist? Pulled back in

a scrunchie? Classic.

FLOTUS Hillary

Demanding an Office in the West Wing

Let's redecorate!

(Don't shut me away where those

Texans were staying.)

Bill of Health

Hill's universal

health-care plan died. But just wait

for Obamacare...

FLOTUS Hillary

FLOTUS in Spring

Alone in a new

office. Outside, interns buzz.

O, to be queen bee...

FLOTUS in Winter

Campaign promises

fade. Wedding vows too are snows

evaporating...

FLOTUS Hillary

"We Are the President"

Winds of scandal blow.

The new dew on a blue dress.

What is a husband?

1998

FLOTUS crusades for
young women. POTUS loves them
too much. Lewinsky.

FLOTUS Hillary

Starr-crossed Lovers

We lingered once in

the rose garden. White House wilts

slowly. Impeachment.

Blue Dress Grievance

O, Tripp, where are your

tapes? Prez is down. Starr's above.

And I am alone.

FLOTUS Hillary

Glass Ceiling Grievance

O, Oval Office!

My term yet? Let my hubby

retire to his sax.

4

Capitol Hill Hill

A Glimpse of New York's New Senator

What solid cankle

peeks beneath yonder pant? It

is hers. Hillary's.

On the Senate Race

"**T**he most difficult
decisions I've made were to
stay married and run."

Capitol Hill Hill

CV Hillary

Wellesley and Yale Law.

First Lady of Arkansas.

FLOTUS (LOL!), et al.

"Rich People, God Bless Us"

"We are going to

take things from you on behalf

of the common good."

Capitol Hill Hill

Fiscal Crisis Hillary

"America, sink

or swim? We can't simply catch

our breath. We must swim."

How Does She Do It?

"**I** have a million

ideas . . . And the easiest

food is pizza." LOL.

Capitol Hill Hill

Candidate Hillary

Campaigns are long; wins,

fleeting. Pantsuited and brave,

Hill, she ain't leaving!

"I'm in. And I'm in to Win."

Finally my turn!

I'll toss in 14 million.

No biggie. I'm in!

Capitol Hill Hill

Pastoral Hill

A long campaign trail

stretches out. Hill's like a horse.

(Work, not show, friend says.)

Pruning the Bushes

"It took a Clinton

to clean up after first Bush...

Might take another..."

Capitol Hill Hill

"I Grew Up in a Middle-Class Family in the Middle of America in the Middle of the Last Century"

Now rich, middle-aged,

Hill aches for that shrinking class.

Taking sides is hard!

Conceding the Primary
in Public

"Life too short, time too

precious, stakes too high to dwell

on what might have been ..."

Capitol Hill Hill

Conceding the Primary in Private

❯? Y? Y? Y? Y? Y?

Y? Y? Y? Y? Y? Y? Y?

Y? Y? Y? Y? Y?

18 Million Cracks

"**A**lthough we were not
able to shatter that glass,
light is shining through."

Capitol Hill Hill

5

Secretary Hillary

BlackBerry Hillary

I'm preceded by

some gurl called Condoleezza?

LOL LMAO.

Double Standard Hillary

"**W**hich designers I

prefer? Would you ever ask

a man that question?"

Secretary Hillary

Drinking Contest
Against McCain

In Estonia,

John keeps pouring vodka shots.

He thought he'd beat me?

Hilli-buster

She's tired. She's over-
tired. She is Obama-tired.
Quelle Secretary.

Secretary Hillary

A Fan Speaks

I like everything

she has ever done! Except

maybe Benghazi.

Inpatient Hillary

Treatment of clot in

transverse venous sinus. (Not

intern! Internist.)

Text to Angela Merkel

❯ingrati8

urself? Be real, gurl. YOLO.

Next up: totes POTUS.

6

Pantsuit Interlude

13 Ways of Looking
at a Pantsuit

If a pantsuit is

being worn, it is being

worn by Hillary.

Among twenty suits

the only moving thing was

Hillary's campaign.

Pantsuit Interlude

Houndstooth? Herringbone?

Of what is Hill's pantsuit made?

Love? Power? Promise?

Bill and Hillary

are one. Billary and pant-

suit are also one.

Pantsuit Interlude

Can't you see pantsuits

filling the Oval Office?

(Carpet has been cleaned.)

I do not know which

to prefer: a suited or

scrunchied Hillary.

Pantsuit Interlude

She rode o'er New York

beneath cracking glass ceilings.

So did her pantsuit.

It was Election

Day all year. Hillary was

blue in a blue suit.

Pantsuit Interlude

Pantsuit, BlackBerry.

Having lost once, she followed

suit. Behind Barack.

She was of three minds.

Like a pantsuit thus comprised:

blouse, jacket, trousers.

Pantsuit Interlude

Come a long way from

headbands, scrunchies. Here she is:

bob, pantsuit, dark shades.

If there are cankles,

one can't know. What is "cankle"

in wide-leg trousers?

Pantsuit Interlude

Pantsuit is moving.

Hillary must be moving.

Primary is soon.

7

Hopeful Hillary

Stay-at-Home Hill

What now? Sit around.

Save elephants. (They are not

Republican, right?)

Hillary's Existential Crisis

What's democracy?

Power? Majority vote?

"YOLO!" Shut up, Bill.

Hopeful Hillary

Empty Nest Hillary

Sent Bill on errands...

Waiting for Chelsea to call...

Soft scrambling eggs...

Audacity of Hillary

Hope, Arkansas, is

far. The kid calls me Grandma.

Can I have it all?

Hopeful Hillary

"I Have Absolutely No Interest in Running for President Again"

? ? ? ? ?

? ? ? ? ? ? ?

? ? ? ? ?

Unidentified Flying Object Thrown at Hillary

It was not, in fact,

a bat. She ain't George Dubya,

and yet, "déjà shoe."

Hopeful Hillary

Flip-Flop Hillary

They love me. They love

me not. They love me. They love

me not. They love me . . .

Six Secretaries of State Became Presidents...

Jefferson. Monroe.

Madison. Q. Adams. Van

Buren. Buchanan...

Hopeful Hillary

She Announces...Finally

I'm running for prez!

Should I have kept those thirty

thousand ditched e-mails?

Ovary Office Hillary

It takes ovaries!

Sisterhood of traveling

pantsuit: forward, march!

Hopeful Hillary

Running Mate Blind Dates

Should it be Warner?

O'Malley? Kaine? Gillibrand?

Awkward like prom! LOL.

The Contenders

Jeb, you stand no chance.

Chris Christie, you still in this?

Trump . . . just keep talking.

Hopeful Hillary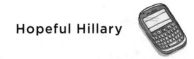

The First First Husband of the United States

Breeze blows through empty

West Wing. The White House awaits

Billary: Part Two.

Hillary of the United States

January frost.

Will HOTUS be moving to

the Oval Office?

Hopeful Hillary

Notes

This book could not have been written without inspiration drawn from Li Po, Tu Fu, Kobayashi Issa, Robert Frost, Wallace Stevens, and Carl Bernstein.

All language within quotation marks are—more or less—true quotations. Some have been shortened or abbreviated based on syllable constraints. However, not to the author's knowledge has Bill Clinton ever exclaimed, proclaimed, or even voiced calmly the expression "YOLO!"

Epigraph

http://blogs.chicagotribune.com/files/hillaryclintonthesis-ocr.pdf

Meeting a Bully

Carl Bernstein, *A Woman in Charge* (New York: Vintage, 2008), 28.

"The Best Tool You Can Give a Child Is a Shovel"

Hillary Rodham Clinton, *It Takes a Village* (New York: Simon & Schuster, 1996), 136–137. This morose chapter heading in *It Takes a Village* actually has a well-intentioned explanation! "My father's approach was vintage Hugh Rodham. When I was facing a problem, he would look me straight in the eyes and ask, 'Hillary, how are you going to dig yourself out of this one?' His query always brought to mind a shovel. That image stayed with me, and over the course of my life I have reached for mental, emotional, and spiritual shovels of various sizes and shapes."

Hillary Stands by Her Man

Carl Bernstein, *A Woman in Charge* (New York: Vintage, 2008), 26.

Hill-Billies

Hillary Clinton, interview by Katie Couric, *Dateline NBC*, April 16, 2004, www.nbcnews.com/id/4757422/ns/dateline_nbc-newsmakers/t/hillary -clinton-talks-politics-future/#.VShaKmbMDS4.

POTUS on Hillary

Bill as quoted on this profile of Hillary, http://clinton2.nara.gov/WH/ glimpse/firstladies/html/hc42.html. "We have a First Lady of many talents… who most of all can bring people together around complex and difficult issues to hammer out consensus and get things done."

"I'm Undaunted in My Quest to Amuse Myself by Constantly Changing My Hair"

HRC's BrainyQuote page, http://www.brainyquote.com/quotes/quotes/h/ hillarycli102223.html. The quote is often attributed without citation to HRC.

"We Are the President"

HRC's Wikiquote page, http://en.wikiquote.org/wiki/Hillary_Rodham _Clinton. There is some question over whether HRC actually said the words attributed to her or not.

On the Senate Race

Hillary Rodham Clinton, *Living History* (New York: Simon & Schuster, 2003), 506.

"Rich People, God Bless Us"

The title is from HRC's response to Bill O'Reilly in 2008 when he said, "I'm not a middle-class family, I'm a rich guy," after she outlined her plans to help the middle class. Full quote: "Rich people, God bless us. We deserve all the opportunities to make sure our country and our blessings continue to the next generation." http://www.foxnews.com/story/ 2008/05/01/hillary-clinton-sits-down-with-bill-oreilly.

The haiku itself is derived from "San Francisco rolls out red carpet for the Clintons," Associated Press, June 28, 2004.

Fiscal Crisis Hillary

Hillary Rodham Clinton, op-ed, "Let's Keep People in Their Homes," *Wall Street Journal*, September 25, 2008, http://online.wsj.com/news/articles/SB122230767702474045.

How Does She Do It?

The quote is a composite of two sources:
http://www.boston.com/news/nation/articles/2007/10/11/clinton_vows_to_check_executive_power
http://www.cbsnews.com/news/clinton-fights-back-tears

"I'm in. And I'm in to Win."

From HRC's announcement that she would run in 2008, http://www.cnn.com/2007/POLITICS/01/20/clinton.announcement/index.html?eref=yahoo.

Pruning the Bushes

www.cnn.com/2008/POLITICS/01/31/dem.debate.transcript

"I Grew Up in a Middle-Class Family in the Middle of America in the Middle of the Last Century"

www.presidency.ucsb.edu/ws/index.php?pid=77051

18 Million Cracks

HRC's concession speech in the primary for the 2008 election, www.nytimes.com/2008/06/07/us/politics/07text-clinton.html?pagewanted=all&_r=0.

Double Standard Hillary

Oh, snap! http://www.huffingtonpost.com/2010/12/02/hillary-clinton-style_n_791358.html.

A Fan Speaks

Hillary fan Morgan Geisert, in author interview. Brooklyn, New York. 2014.

"I Have Absolutely No Interest in Running for President Again"

... Really: http://abcnews.go.com/video/playerIndex?id=8824513.

Unidentified Flying Object Thrown at Hillary

Thank you, *New York Daily News*, for this important story, and for the phrase "déjà shoe."

About the Author and Illustrator

VERA G. SHAW was born in the United States, but her soul resides in a Japanese garden. By day, she chops wood and carries water; by night, she weds the complexity of haiku to the simplicity of American politics. A poet of many shifting selves, layered as a lily blooming on a still pond, she lives in Clinton Hill, Brooklyn, with two cats named Democracy and Tu-Fu, respectively.

EMMY REIS was born and raised in Japan between her Japanese mother and American father. Following her older sister who is a fine artist in New York, she moved to the city and graduated from Parsons The New School for Design in 2013 with a BFA. Emmy is currently based in New York and Kyoto, running around drawing and painting in her two favorite places on earth.

ABOUT TWELVE

TWELVE

TWELVE was established in August 2005 with the objective of publishing no more than twelve books each year. We strive to publish the singular book, by authors who have a unique perspective and compelling authority. Works that explain our culture; that illuminate, inspire, provoke, and entertain. We seek to establish communities of conversation surrounding our books. Talented authors deserve attention not only from publishers, but from readers as well. To sell the book is only the beginning of our mission. To build avid audiences of readers who are enriched by these works—that is our ultimate purpose.

For more information about forthcoming TWELVE books, please go to www.twelvebooks.com.